My name is Lau... only child and I... mom, who is a single parent

My mum loves me and tries her best with me. I know it is not always easy, but she still smiles at me by the end of the day when we read together

Gen 1:31

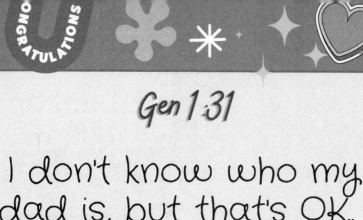

Gen 1:31

I don't know who my dad is, but that's OK..

I know who I am. God made me and He says He made me well.

I am ten years old and like
gymnastics and swimming..

We swim twice a week, as
mum works.

I have gymnsatics at
school, so, at least we don't
have to worry about
getting there.

Ps 139

I like drawing. Mum says I need to practise much more for my drawings to be really good. I carry my book, pencils and crayons everywhere with me. I just like doing it for fun.

Ps 139

I like eating pizza and ice cream and watching movies.

I think I am a very typical little girl.

Ps 139

I have two best friends.
Their names are Maisy and Tammy.

I like my friends.
WE are quite close and take turns to hang out at each other's houses.

Ps 139

We sometimes hang out, and sometimes go to the movies, or just go the mcDonalds'.

Ps 139

I really like it when they visit me, as my mum make very special brownies.

They really ooze with melting chocholate, or caramel.

Ps 139

We normally get to watch anything on Netflix., or Amazon videos.

Ps 139

We like to eat chips, spaghetti bolognaise, or pizza.

We many times have milkshake, or coke with it.

Ps 139

My friends are now starting to ask for diet cold drinks.

My mum says she is not too keen on us having diet stuff, as we are too young.

Ps139

I love it when we have a sleepover. We play games, talk and just sit together.

Ps 139

We all end up wearing our onesies and just have fun..

Ps 139

We like hot chocolate and sometimes drink a warm spicy apple drink.

Ps 139

Sometimes we do each other's hair, or paint our nails..

Ps 139

We sometimes lie on the bed and compare ourselves. We only compare legs, bums and tums.

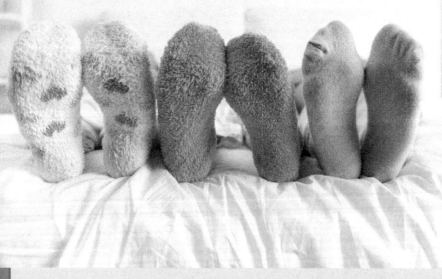

Psalms 139

I don't mind when we compare ourselves as I know that I am OK.

Ps 139

I don't like it when my friends don't like parts of themselves and sometimes tells me how they hate themselves.

Ps 139

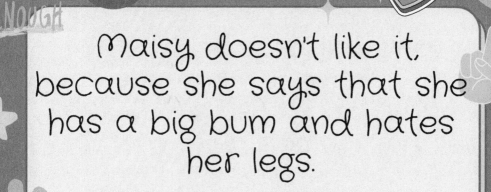

Maisy doesn't like it, because she says that she has a big bum and hates her legs.

Psalms 139

I think Maisy's bum is just the right size for her. If it was any smaller, her trousers would fall off. Her waist is quite narrow.

Her legs are very long and thin. I don't know why she doesn't like them, Tammy and I encourage her that they are perfect.

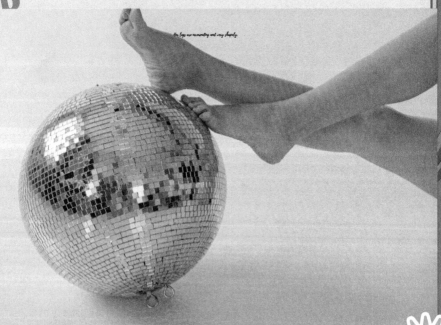

Her legs are very long and very shapely.

Ps 139

Maisy now say that she is not eating all the stuff we always have.

She brings herself some YLCD bars and shakes, but we don't make a fuss of it.

Pg 139

This makes it a bit a̶k̶eward for Tammy and myself, as we feel we can't enjoy our pizza and chips as much, when Maisy just eat one YLCD bar with water.

Pg 139

It almost make me feel guilty for wanting to eat normally

I refuse to feel that way

God made me special, I have a purpose, I will not feel guilty for being normal.

Jer 29:11

I always try to encourage them and tell them how beautiful they are.

I like them, and I like me.

Ps 139

I've started this game where we tell each other what we admire about each other and why the other person is so amazing.

Each one gets a turn and you have to be honest. You can't just say make something up..

Ps 139

I really like playing the game, becasue it seems that Tammy and Maisy always feel better aterwards and have more smiles.

Ps 139

I can almost say in
that moment, they like
themselves too.

Ps 139

I like it when they are happy and stop hating themselves.

I think people sometimes focus too much on themselves and their flaws and stop enjoying life..

Ps 139

I belief that we should always believe that we are great with all ours hearts., but that doesn't seem the way

Ps 139

I think it is nesassary to encourage our friends, because they will more likely open up to you, than their parents, or teacher.

Ps 139

We know our friends.
best. we know when
they are happy, or sad.
Our friends carry their
hearts on their sleeves.

Ps 139

I do encourage Tammy
and Maisy to come to
gymnastics and swimming
with me and just enjoy
themselves and
enjoy life.

Ps 139

It is worth keeping an eye on the shy kids too.

They can easily be missed. You don't know what is going on in their lives.

Ps 139

I hang out with Shy, Whitney and Olivia

I don't want them to fall through the gaps. No one knows how they feel, as they are so shy, that not many people bother speaking to them..

Ps 139

I don't want anyone to dislike themselves so much that they want to hurt themselves.

I think we should help each other and make ourselves better.

Ps 139

Sometimes it is worth just meeting up with someone to let them talk. It always helps when I am feeling sad

I also like going for a bike ride, or a walk on the beach. It always cheers me up.

Ps 139

What cheers you up? What makes you feel better when you feel miserable and sad?

It is quite normal to feel miserable and sad, but mum always says to not wallow in it.

Feel it, face it, and get over it.

Ps 139

What is your happy place?

Do you like to feed the ducks? Do you have dogs that you just hug and talk to and instantly feel better?

Ps 139

Do you have a happy place
where you go to?

To just remove yourself
from your situation, just for
a little bit, so you can deal
with your emotions?

Ps 139

I like to read the Bible and say out loud what God says about me.

I also study myself in the mirror and tell myself what God says about me.
I like myself.

Ps 139

I like me..

Mummy said that it is important to like yourself, otherwise how do you expect other to like you?

I'm not sure, let's look at each bit carefully and then make a decision.

Ps 139

I know not everybody likes me. I think it is more important that I like myself.

I spend a lot of time with myself. I have to live with myself all the time!

Ps 139

My hair is brown, maybe a bit mousy, but it's not too dark, and not too light.

Its perfectly in the middle.

A little bit like Goldilocks' porridge, just right.

Psalms 139

My hair is curly, maybe a bit messy. It keeps my head warm and makes me look nice, I think I like it.

Ps 139

have blue eyes with normal eyelashes and eyebrows.

They seem to work ok.. I can see everything I need to.

So, I like my eyes.

Ps 139

My nose is a bit stubby. A bit small, but I don't need a big nose.

My nose does what the box says, I can breathe through it and smell all the lovely spices, food and flowers.

Ps 139

I think I like my nose.

It is fit for purpose, as my mum always says when customers complain.

Ps 139

My mouth has two lips.
My mouth can smile, laugh
and cry. I can eat with
my mouth and kiss.

My mouth is a house for
my teeth and tongue.

Ps 139

My tongue can taste all the lovely flavours in cold drinks and hot chocolate. It can taste sour lemons, so I think my mouth works like it should.

Ps 139

I can stick out my tongue
and lick an ice cream, so I
think my tongue works well.

Ps 139

My teeth can bite and chew my favourite food.

I brush my teeth twice a day

Ps 139

They might not be perfectly straight and shiny white, but they work well.

I think, I like my mouth.

Ps 139

I have a good strong chin.
There are no dimples, or
anything, but I like it plain
anyway.

I like my chin.

Ps 139

My neck is straight, not quite as long as an ostrich, but I suppose, that is a good thing.

It can turn both ways, nod up and down and carry my head.

Ps 139

I think that is all it is supposed to do, so it's a good neck. I think I like my neck a lot.

Ps 139

My shoulders are a bit broad for a girl, as I like swimming and gymnastics.

I sometimes struggle a bit to get pretty girly shirts, with pretty pictures on it, to fit well.

Ps 139

But, my shoulders work well.

I just have to get a bit looser shirts, or like to learn different type of shirts. Shirts without shoulders fits awesome. .

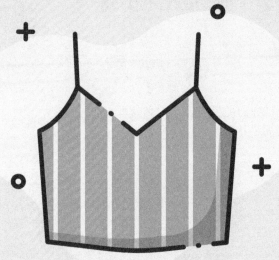

Ps 139

I can turn my arms all the way round like a helicopter.

My shoulders hold my arms and my arms work well. I think I like my shoulders.

My arms and hands help me hang on the monkey bars. I can swing around and have a lot of fun.

Psalms 139

I can also hang on the big rings in gymnastics. I can swim by just using my arms.

I think I like my arms.

Psalms 139

My elbows bend in the right direction. They are quite strong, as I can do push ups in gymnastics.

I think I like my elbows.

Ps 139

The biggest reason I like my hand is because it can hold a lot of things. I can carry my toys, my phone, and ice cream.

Ps 139

I can carry plates with food and use tools, like a knife and fork to get the food in my mouth. I can draw nice and enjoy using crayons.

Pg 139

The skin on my fingers is a bit dry, so I need to put a lot of cream and body balm on it to make it look decent, but, I think I like my hands.

They are very useful.

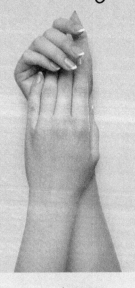

Ps 139

My body is tall and
maybe a bit lanky

Mum says I will still fill
out but I don't mind I
like my body. It works
well.

My body does exactly what it needs to, and it carries my arms, neck and legs, holding me all together.

It works, so I like me

Ps 139

My chest is a bit broad but it's OK. I think it is from the swimming.

I can breathe well, so my chest is OK.

I like my chest.

Ps 139

My back is a bit broad but it's OK. My back covers the back of all my internal organs. There are muscles in it and I think it works well.

I like my back.

Ps 139

My tummy is not flat. Some girls wants very flat stomachs and keep doing situps, but I think it is normal to have a bit of a bump, boys have it too.

We've got stuff in there!!

I like my tummy

Ps 139

My bum might be a bit small. I don't mind too much. I can sit on it, and it holds my jeans up. I think that is all it is supposed to do.

I like my bum.

Ps 139

My legs are a bit short and stodgy, but I just have to jump higher and run faster.
I still get where I need to go.

Ps 139

. My legs kick nice and it helps me to swim fast from one side to the other side of the pool.

I like my legs.

Ps 139

My knees are a bit knock knees, but I don't mind. It is easy to stretch out doing splits and knock knees dances.

I can do the new tick tock "Megan knees" very well. Haha. I enjoy that. My legs work well, so I like them.

Ps 139

I have lovely feet.

Five toes on each. My
feet helps me to walk,
run and jump.

Ps 139

My mom says I've got
monkey toes, as I can
climb trees well. I don't
mind my toes and feet
works well.

I like them.

Ps 139

When I look in the mirror, I see what God says, And it was made well. Every body part works like it should.

I was made well.

Gen 1:31

I might not have a model perfect body and in the best porportions, but it is mine.

This is me.

Be your own kind of BEAUTIFUL

Ps 139

I am not perfect, but there is nothing wrong with me. Everything works well. Everything is where it should be. Sometimes is is worth accepting you for who you are and your body for what it is.

Ps 139

Deal with it. It is all you have There are no spare parts to make you better. Deal with your warts and acne. Some things you can make better, other things you need to accept..

Ps 139

I guarantee that you will feel much happier once you accept. yourself the way God made you and learn to live with it.

Eat well, drink well, do your training, but enjoy life..

Ps 139

Psalms 139

I think it is safe to say
that I like myself.

From the bottom to
the top.

I can even stretch it
and say that, some
times, I actually love
myself.

I think I am
wonderfully put
together. God did a
good job, and I am
proud to say, I am
fearfully and
wonderfully made.

Psalms 139

Psalms 139:14 NKJV

I will praise You, for I am fearfully and wonderfully made; Marvellous are Your works, And that my soul knows very well.

Printed in Great Britain
by Amazon